Original title:
The Endless Summer

Copyright © 2025 Creative Arts Management OÜ
All rights reserved.

Author: Nora Sinclair
ISBN HARDBACK: 978-1-80581-500-6
ISBN PAPERBACK: 978-1-80581-027-8
ISBN EBOOK: 978-1-80581-500-6

Journey into the Light

Sunshine spills on my face,
Sandy toes in a clammy race.
Ice cream drips like sweet confetti,
We laugh so loud, we're not quite steady.

Kites are flying, high on the breeze,
A seagull steals my chips with ease.
The beach ball's lost, where did it go?
But in this glow, who cares? Just flow!

A Dance of Warm Breezes

Breezes twist, they tease our hats,
While crabs dance like little acrobats.
Laughter echoes, waves splash playfully,
Who knew the ocean could be so wily?

Sunburned noses and silly shades,
Beach games turn into comical charades.
Fins are waving, surfboards slide,
In this dance, we take our stride!

Seaside Reveries

Shells and seaweed, scattered treasures,
Finding odd things gives us great measures.
The tide pulls jokes from way out deep,
As giggles roll, we leap and leap.

A hermit crab's wearing a strange hat,
Oh look, there's Dad, chillin' with a cat.
Sunscreen globs, like modern art,
In this silly place, we find a heart!

Boundless Days Ahead

Each morning brings sun-kissed delight,
But who will chase off the comfiest night?
Tanned kids jump, daring the wave,
In this paradise, we're all so brave.

Digging holes to China, it seems,
While plotting big, ambitious schemes.
As day surrenders to the stars,
We laugh so hard, it's truly bizarre!

Unfading Light

In flip-flops we roam, the sun's our best mate,
Ice cream in hand, not a moment too late.
Sand stuck to our feet, oh what a delight,
We laugh and we frolic, from morning to night.

Squirrels run by, with snacks they have found,
While seagulls swoop low, they think they're quite crowned.
With shades on our noses, we look like cool fools,
In this sunny paradise, we break all the rules.

Whispers of Endless Warmth

Bikini tops sag, as we hit the waves hard,
We play like we're kids, and life's our backyard.
Surfboards and laughter, a recipe grand,
We wipe out of style, but still, we'll make plans.

The fries are all gone, but our spirits are high,
With ketchup on faces, we look like the sky.
A tan like a lobster, how do we achieve?
With sunscreen we'd hoped, but oh, can you believe?

Golden Days Ahead

Chasing the sunset with a snack on the run,
We giggle like puppies, oh, life is such fun.
A seagull takes wing, diving right for our fries,
While we munch on old chips, a hilarious surprise.

Our tunes blare so loud, we dance like mad fools,
With colors bright fading, we make our own rules.
Beach balls collide, creating chaos and cheer,
In this never-ending bliss, we find we have no fear.

Celestial Play

Stars sprinkle the sky, in flip-flop ballet,
We chase them like fireflies at the end of the day.
With laughter like waves, crashing soft on the shore,
We scream to the moon, 'Just give us some more!'

Our jokes are like sunshine, they light up our souls,
With sand in our hair, we're achieving our goals.
Who needs the sunset when we've got this spark?
In this land of delight, we're leaving our mark.

Warm Winds of Tomorrow

Warm winds whisper tales of sun,
As sunburnt noses start to run.
A beach ball flies, with squeaky sound,
While seagulls steal our snacks around.

In flip-flops we will shuffle low,
Chasing ice cream that's set to go.
Laughter echoes, waves collide,
While sunscreen sprays like summer pride.

The Horizon's Lullaby

The horizon hums a silly tune,
With beach umbrellas by the moon.
A sandcastle towers, oh so grand,
But crabs declare it's their own land.

As flip-flops squawk with every step,
We dodge the waves, yet still we crept.
A sunhat's veiling goofy grins,
While laughter dances in the winds.

A Tidal Dance of Light

The tide begins its wobbly dance,
As jellyfish float in their trance.
With frisbees flying, laughter rings,
Our hearts revive with summer flings.

A kite takes flight, a rainbow's tease,
As we race crabs and laugh with ease.
Sunbeams stretch across the shore,
While seagulls battle for our score.

Pathways in Sunlight

Pathways shine like golden dreams,
As lemonade flows with icy beams.
We dodge the dog with frisbee bold,
And chase the sunset, bright and gold.

In floppy hats and silly cheer,
We dance with shadows, drawing near.
The day slips on with playful grace,
As laughter fills this sunny space.

Forever in Bloom

Flowers giggle in the sun,
Bees in shades of yellow run.
A tomato wearing shades so bright,
Says, 'Just another day of light!'

The daisies dance with silly grace,
One did a twirl, fell on its face!
The daisies laugh, the tulips cheer,
Let's soak in warmth, it's our time here!

Butterflies in a wild parade,
All upset when the sun does fade.
They whisper secrets, share a joke,
As clouds come in, they start to poke!

This garden's life, a hapless crew,
Frogs in sunglasses, what a view!
Every petal takes a chance,
In this sunshine, we all prance!

Sunkissed Moments

Lemons sip drinks with a cheer,
Sipping sunshine, what a year!
Lollipops with tan lines too,
Join the fun, let's paint in blue!

Ice cream cones begin to melt,
Waffles laugh, their joy is felt.
On the beach, a sandcastle stands,
'Though waves are coming, let's make plans!'

Seagulls steal fries with a squawk,
Chasing crumbs like a silly mock.
Flip flops flutter on the sand,
As sun hats wave, they make a band!

Sunkissed moments, bright and sweet,
Life is a dance, oh what a feat!
Catch the giggles, don't miss a beat,
For days like this, we are complete!

Delights of a Timeless Season

Picnics spread on grassy beds,
Ants bring snacks, our tiny friends.
A cheese wheel rolls, it just can't stop,
While squirrels plot to take the top!

Jokes with ketchup and mustard flow,
Hot dog races, just for show.
Hamburgers giggle, buns in a spin,
And lemonade wears a silly grin.

The sunbeams tickle, laughter grows,
Chasing shadows, anything goes.
Everyone's invited, what a sight,
As we toast marshmallows into the night!

Timeless fun in every bite,
Catch a firefly, hold it tight.
All these snacks and jokes galore,
Make me wish for just one more.

Sunlit Paths

On sunlit paths we skip and hop,
With goofy hats, we never stop.
A squirrel is juggling someone's snack,
While we all laugh, in a playful hack!

Cool breezes tease, can you take it?
Bubbles float and someone fakes it.
Lost my flip flop, now I'm a mess,
But in this warmth, I couldn't care less!

A dance-off with the old oak tree,
Who would win? Just wait and see!
The branches sway, the leaves all clap,
As we twirl around in a silly map.

Endless trails where fun never dies,
Giggling clouds float through the skies.
With every step, we find delight,
In every moment, laughter's bright!

Fields of Forever Gold

In fields where laughter echoes wide,
We roll like tumbleweeds, our pride.
The sun above, a smiling face,
Chases us in this magic place.

Ants in pants and silly hats,
Wiggling like a bunch of cats.
Picnics spread on checkered cloth,
Ice cream drips, oh, what a smoth!

Kites dance high in skies of blue,
With tails that wiggle, just like you.
Backflips, cartwheels, all in play,
While golden beams light up the day.

As dusk falls soft, we like to think,
That lemonade could solve a stink.
With fireflies dancing, we then know,
A night of fun is sure to flow.

The Dance of Fiery Days

When daylight twirls in vibrant hues,
We skip and hop in worn-out shoes.
The heat brings out our silliest grins,
As we all dance and twirl like spins.

Sunscreen slathered, we look quite mad,
With laughter bursting, oh so glad.
Water balloons fly through the air,
Popsicle races, none to spare!

Catch the breeze under palm tree shade,
Sipping slushies, mischief made.
Bubblegum stuck on someone's shoe,
A sticky end is nothing new!

As twilight wraps the world in gold,
We sit together, stories told.
With firelight flickering, we shall say,
"Let's dance like it's a grand ballet!"

Moments That Shine On

In a world of bright and goofy glee,
We laugh so loud, just you and me.
Sandcastles rise while seagulls squawk,
This silly life, it surely rocks!

With lemonade stands on busy streets,
And funny hats that can't be beat.
We chase the ice cream truck nearby,
With dreams of sundaes 'neath the sky.

Our bicycles parade in the sun,
Racing wildly, oh what fun!
With squeaky brakes and wheels that spin,
We wobble 'round but always win.

As stars peek out from dusky skies,
We share our secrets, silly lies.
And though these moments won't last long,
They shine like notes in our fond song.

Serene Days Adrift

On lazy days, we float like boats,
In dreamy fields, we share our quotes.
A breeze that tickles, whispers low,
We giggle at all the laughs we know.

With sun hats large and toes in sand,
We make the silliest jokes unplanned.
The ocean waves clap like fans,
As we build castles, oh so grand!

Chasing clouds that drift on by,
In skies with colors, oh my, oh my!
A frisbee lands in a neighbor's yard,
Then runs away, oh, that's just hard!

When evening comes, we'll dance and sway,
Under the stars, "Hip-hip-hooray!"
With all our fun, we watch the sun,
Fade away, but oh, what a run!

Solstice Serenade

The sun's a cheeseball, bright and bold,
Waving at ice cream cones, oh, so cold.
Bikinis dancing, the breeze in play,
Seagulls squawking, they make my day.

Lemonade laughter, spills on the sand,
Flip-flop symphony, let's form a band.
Sunglasses perched like a regal crow,
Who knew warmth could steal the show?

Basking in Limelight

Sunshine has auditions, take the stage,
With a wink, it sets the world ablaze.
Wobbly chairs on the porch just laugh,
While squirrels practice their acrobat craft.

Ice pops droop, they're melting away,
Just like my plans for a clear, chill day.
Yet sun-kissed giggles ride every wave,
The beach is a stage, and I'm feeling brave!

Days That Never Fade

Morning coffee's a tickle fight,
With the sun, it seems oh-so right.
Mismatched socks walk on warm ground,
Making a fashion statement profound.

Flip-flops chatter, pass a grin,
As ice cream drips, we start to spin.
The calendar laughs, it's gone too far,
In this haze, we're all rock stars!

Sunkissed Memories

Picnics undone, ants in a row,
They think they rule, but we steal the show.
Jumping in puddles, but wait it's dry,
Splashing our secrets, oh me, oh my!

The hammock's a cloud, and I'm in a dream,
Floating away like a sunbeam's gleam.
With each silly thought, let's toast with cheer,
These moments are magic, or maybe a beer!

Endless Days of Sunlight

Sunscreen slathered from head to toes,
Ice cream drips on a nose that glows.
Lizards sunbathe, adopting a pose,
While seagulls squawk, stealing fries as prose.

Beach balls bouncing with joyful noise,
Flip-flops flapping, a pair of toys.
Sandcastles crumble, oh what a choice,
Mermaids giggle in carefree poise.

Kites are soaring, children run wild,
Tickled by laughter, just like a child.
Bikini tops pulling, no moment mild,
Sunburned dads keep on dancing, beguiled.

What's for lunch? A picnic surprise,
Sandwiches melting under sunny skies.
Life's a game, and the fun never dies,
Endless laughter is where the heart flies.

Radiant Horizons

Chasing shadows, we race through the day,
Beach umbrellas like mushrooms in May.
Tanning our toes, then we run to play,
While ice cubes melt in the heat's dismay.

Clouds are scarce, like a missing sock,
The ocean's our friend, tickling our dock.
A sunburned crab does a funny rock,
As kids scream for joy, on a laughing mock.

Picnic ants set up a surprise feast,
While the breeze whispers jokes to say the least.
A dolphin jumps, turning into a beast,
As we grin with delight that will never cease.

Heatwaves dance, making visions sway,
With lemonade cheers to brighten the way.
Life's a carnival, come join the fray,
In moments of laughter, we choose to play.

Infinite Warmth

The sun yawns wide, waking the day,
Shorts on legs that dare to sway.
Sandy toes in a lighthearted ballet,
While waves crash in a playful display.

Picnic baskets spilling bright treats,
Seagulls dive-bombing, oh, such feats!
Kids run amok, skipping in beats,
Sandmen built, wearing gumdrop seats.

Barefoot races, who's the real champ?
Chasing ice cream trucks, setting up camp.
Sunburned noses, like a plump lamp,
Our laughter echoes, glittering like a stamp.

Bonfires at dusk, marshmallows roast,
Friends share stories, each one a boast.
Under bright stars, we'll dance and toast,
To the funny moments we cherish most.

Golden Hours Stretching

Sunrise giggles, a brand-new day,
The world's a stage where we all play.
Golden rays lead our merry way,
As children build dreams in a sunlit array.

Hats on heads, backwards for flair,
Holding popsicles, flavors to share.
Running in circles without a care,
While laughter floats freely in warm summer air.

Shuffleboard tiles, a clash of delight,
Old folks grumbling, "We'll show them tonight!"
The hammock sways under giggles so bright,
As sunset spills colors, a dazzling sight.

Firefly dances, as stars appear,
The sounds of joy are all we hear.
With every tick, we hold moments near,
In a season of fun, year after year.

Solstice Dreams

Sunshine spills like lemonade,
Ice cream trucks parade and serenade.
Flip-flops squeak on sandy ground,
As seagulls plot their food around.

Picnic ants march in a line,
While kids compete in sunbeam shine.
Beach balls bounce, a wild dance,
Sunscreen battles, no second chance.

Tanned and laughing, cheeks so pink,
Coconut drinks with tiny blinks.
In a hammock, dreams take flight,
Life's a giggle, pure delight.

In the Heart of July

Fireworks fizzle like bad jokes,
Grill smoke mingles with rad folks.
Sizzling sausages do the twist,
While lemonade gives summer a kiss.

Misplaced sunglasses on a dog,
A sun-soaked game of leapfrog.
Chasing ice cream on a hot chase,
Turns into a whipped cream race.

Popsicle drips like melting dreams,
While playful pranks collect their memes.
Time slows down, on laughter's wing,
July sings out—oh, what a fling!

Shores of Radiance

Waves crash in a sassy splash,
As surfers practice their best crash.
Beach hats bounce to reggae tunes,
Sunbathers form a blanket commune.

Sandcastles rise with royal flair,
While dogs dig holes without a care.
Kites soar high, as children squeal,
The beach is lit, it's a zany reel.

Shells collect stories, sun-kissed and bright,
Footprints wash away, out of sight.
The day drifts on, a nautical jest,
In the shore's embrace, we find our rest.

Twilight's Eternal Glow

Fireflies blink in a winking race,
As marshmallows roast and glow with grace.
Crispy treats fall from sticky hands,
While laughter echoes, life just expands.

A blanket fort springs up at dusk,
With dreams unfurling, woven husk.
Stars peek out in playful glee,
As shadows dance beneath a tree.

Magic moments in a twilight mix,
The clock ticks slow, no need for tricks.
In this warm hug, night takes its flow,
A sunset giggle, a radiant show.

Time Suspended in Brightness

The ice cream melts, oh what a sight,
A sticky hand, a face so bright.
Chasing seagulls, we trip and fall,
But laughing hard, we stand up tall.

In the splash zone of a fountain we play,
Drenched and giggling, what a display!
A sun hat flies, caught in the breeze,
We run like kids, feeling so free.

Sandcastle towers lean and sway,
With seashells gathered on the way.
Splat! A friend takes a face full of wave,
We laugh so hard, our sides we crave.

Bouncing beach balls, a friendly fight,
Sunburned noses gleaming in light.
Time feels weird, a funny twist,
In this blissful haze, who could resist?

Laughter Under the Sun

Picnics sprawled on checkered cloth,
Ants march in, we yell, "Get lost!"
Sandwiches squished, we dance around,
With crumbs and giggles all abound.

A game of frisbee, oh what a throw,
It lands in the ice cream, oh no!
We wipe our hands and take a bite,
Sweet and sticky, what a delight.

Palm trees sway, a palm frond hat,
Sporting styles that leave us flat.
Rolling on sand, we laugh and spin,
Sandy hair, let the fun begin!

Sunsets glow, a vibrant show,
We pose like models, striking a blow.
With sand in our shoes, we bid adieu,
But the laughter stays, and the joy just grew.

Immortal Light

Sunglasses on, we're rockstars today,
Walking around in a silly array.
A lemonade stand, we dance with zest,
This endless vibe, we're feeling blessed.

A slip 'n slide with friends in tow,
Like dolphins splashing, let's steal the show!
Who's got the better splash, we compete,
Wet and wild, oh, can't be beat.

Chasing butterflies, they lead the way,
We tumble and giggle, the joys display.
Pick up a conch, it's our crown for now,
Regal in laughter, we take a bow.

Fireflies blink as the evening calls,
Swapping stories, the glow enthralls.
In this timeless place, we find our delight,
With immortal joy, forever in light.

The Whisper of Sunbeams

Whispers echo where shadows dwell,
A tickle of sun, oh can't you tell?
We dance with daisies, all in a whirl,
Hopping like frogs, laughter's our pearl.

Kites soaring high, we give them a chase,
Sudden swoops, and the wind is our race.
Faces alight, we shout and cheer,
Caught in the breeze, no worry here.

Bubbles float, what a curious sight,
We chase them down as they take flight.
Popped and giggled, it's pure delight,
This playful spirit, oh what a height!

As daylight fades, we build a fire,
Telling stories, our hearts inspire.
Under the stars, we hold on tight,
To this sweet magic, our endless night.

Embracing the Horizon

Sunburnt feet on sizzling sand,
Ice cream melting in my hand.
Seagulls squawking, what a sight,
Chasing shadows, oh, what delight.

Beach balls bounce with cheerful glee,
Waves crash down, just like me.
Flip-flops flying, laughter loud,
Hiding under the sun, so proud.

Sandy toes and giggling friends,
This joy just never seems to end.
Kites are tangled in a tree,
Oh, save me from this sticky spree!

As the sun sets, colors blend,
We're all kids, no need to pretend.
Chasing dreams as night reveals,
Tomorrow's fun is what it steals.

A Season's Timeless Whisper

Barefoot walking, on the street,
Munching corn that's oh-so-sweet.
Popsicle drips on my shirt,
Sticky giggles, this is my hurt.

Picnics spread on plaid blankets,
Sipping drinks from old canteens.
Bee stings and laughter combined,
Riddles, pranks, what a nice grind!

The ice cream truck, a joyous sound,
We dash and spin, so unbound.
Chasing fireflies, in a daze,
Counting stars for endless days.

Each sunset brings a goofy dance,
Like we're living in a trance.
Here's a splatter of bright fun,
Everlasting under the sun.

Horizon's Embrace

The sun peeks out, it's time to play,
Sipping lemonade, fading away.
Snorkels ready, what will we find?
A sock, a shoe – they all unwind.

Slides that exit into the pool,
Kids laughing, oh, what a drool.
Finding crabs, making a fuss,
"Hey, that's my sandwich!" with a rush.

Sandcastles towering, one falls down,
"Time for victory!" I wear the crown.
A beach ball bonk on my head gives me cheer,
Rolling around, squeals of glee are near.

As dusk arrives, fireflies blink,
Telling stories about the stink.
With doodles in sand, under the stars,
Who knew summer could be so bizarre?

Glow of the Everlasting

Waking early, the sun's a treat,
Fish tacos and warm, toasted wheat.
Singing loudly on the boardwalk,
Our dance moves? Just an awkward talk.

Sun hats big, like mushroom caps,
Crafting laughs from silly mishaps.
With sunscreen slathered thickly on,
Who cares about a little con?

Chasing waves and splashing in style,
Building forts that last a short while.
Why did we bring that giant float?
Oh dear, now it won't stay afloat!

Evenings filled with marshmallow roasts,
Ghost stories told by overenthused hosts.
In this glow, let the fun spill,
We cherish moments, laughter's thrill.

A Canvas of Warmth

Sunshine splatters on the floor,
Like lemonade spilled from a store.
Children chase goats, always in flight,
While ice cream drips, oh what a sight!

Flip-flops squeak on the sidewalk,
As neighbors gather for their talk.
A cat naps on a sprinkler's spray,
While dogs dig holes, come what may!

The grill's ablaze with sizzling sound,
As burgers bounce on the ground.
A lawn chair wobbles with each sway,
But who cares? It's a perfect day!

Balloons soar high, drifting afar,
While dad swears he's not a bad star.
With sunburned noses and laughter loud,
Summer's canvas draws its crowd!

When Shadows Dance

Shadows stretch and twist with glee,
As people chase them, wild and free.
Laughter echoes, a joyful prance,
While kids try to catch their shadow's dance!

The sun plays peek-a-boo with trees,
As squirrels plot their nutty fees.
Frog leaps away with a slippery slide,
While children giggle and run wide-eyed!

Old folks lounge with a iced cold drink,
Setting the mood, here's a wink.
Flip-flops flop, a fashion faux pas,
But hey, it's summer—who cares, ha-ha?

A kite zips high, a colorful show,
While parents wave from below.
The sun dips low—time to prance,
And join the shadows in their dance!

Luminosity Unbound

Stars wink down like shiny coins,
While a dog barks at phantom phones.
The hammock sways, a gentle tease,
As grandpa snores, oh how he wheezes!

Fireflies blink in a sparkly game,
While laughter bursts like wild confetti flame.
A picnic blanket spills with treats,
As ants march in for stolen sweets!

The moon plays tricks, a gleaming grin,
While friends debate where to begin.
Is it the juice or dad's old hat,
That makes us giggle and chat like that?

With lemonade served in mismatched cups,
And tickles traded in playful ups.
Life's bright glow is seldom profound,
It's all just a form of luminosity unbound!

Endless Days of Gold

Glistening sands beneath our toes,
Where the air is sweet as summer's prose.
With laughter bubbling like cool brook,
Who needs a plan? Let's read a book!

Ice cream towers atop a cone,
Drips like a rainstorm, overblown.
Boys plan a heist for a stolen pop,
While girls paint nails till the night won't stop!

Bees buzz loud around the blooms,
While belly laughs fill all the rooms.
A lemonade stand run by kids with style,
Leads to giggles, and a sticky trial!

As daylight wanes, we'll sit in a row,
And watch the sky put on a show.
With endless gold in our hearts to hold,
Forever we'll dance in these days of gold!

Forever in Bloom

In gardens where the daisies chatter,
The bees improvise a lively patter.
The sun invites a goofy dance,
While grasshoppers plot their next big chance.

Bright tulips wear their Sunday best,
While squirrels debate their nutty quest.
A daffodil shows off its flair,
As bunnies hop without a care.

The daisies giggle, the roses sigh,
While sunbeams tickle both you and I.
Nature sings its merry tune,
Beneath the watchful eye of the moon.

With petals swirling in the breeze,
The flowers whisper, "Life's a tease."
In this blooming funny spree,
Who knew nature held the key?

Beneath the Eternal Sky

Beneath the sky so blue and wide,
Clouds play hide and seek, they glide.
A parrot cracks a joke so loud,
While witty sunbeams form a crowd.

The trees gossip with the breeze,
A squirrel rustles, "Don't sneeze, please!"
With kites that dance like they know how,
And ducks that quack a silly vow.

The sun takes selfies with the moon,
As critters line up for a cartoon.
A jester's hat upon a crow,
Life's just a stage, and it's a show!

With laughter echoing across the land,
Joy and silliness go hand in hand.
Beneath this endless, playful dome,
Nature giggles, and calls it home.

Against the Cascading Waves

The waves giggle as they crash and sprout,
With sandcastles holding a goofy route.
A crab dons shades and struts around,
While seashells whisper laughter profound.

Surfers tumble in a twisty spree,
As dolphins leap with glee from the sea.
A starfish makes a sand angel lay,
While seagulls chat about the day.

With vibrant kites soaring overhead,
Each splash is laughter, precisely spread.
Barnacles in a conga line,
In this amusing shoreline, all is fine!

The sun dips low, a comical sprite,
Painting the waves in soft twilight.
Against this scene of splashes and foam,
Laughter echoes, it feels like home.

In the Warmth of Infinity

In the warmth where sun rays tickle toes,
Ticklish giggles feel like a rose.
With ice cream drips and messy grins,
Joy dances in, as summer begins.

With frisbees flyin' at sunny speeds,
As laughter grows among the weeds.
A cat in shades lounges, quite the sight,
While sunglasses claim it's a "cool" night.

Picnics bloom with whimsical treats,
As ants march in to steal some sweets.
A kite soars high, on a string so fine,
While laughter mingles with a glass of wine.

As starlit skies come into view,
We toast to the joy and nonsense too.
In this infinite embrace of fun,
We find our hearts, and summer's just begun!

Days that Never Fade

The sun is up, it won't come down,
We dance around in silly crowns.
Ice cream drips down on our toes,
We're laughing hard; who really knows?

Beach balls bounce with joyous cheer,
We surf the waves, no hint of fear.
A seagull steals my tasty fry,
A snack attack—the cheeky guy!

Flip-flops flying, running wild,
The heat's a gift; we gasp and smiled.
Sunglasses on, we post for likes,
Though sunscreen smears make us lookikes.

So here we are, each sun-kissed face,
With goofy grins, we claim our space.
This endless fun is not a tease,
Just silly hearts caught in the breeze.

Eternal Shoreline Dreams

On sandy shores, where seagulls wail,
We build a castle, not for sale.
A wave comes crashing, ruins the fun,
But we just laugh, we've barely begun!

With bucket hats and shades galore,
We hunt for treasures on the floor.
A driftwood stick? A fishy shoe?
We've got the best finds, who needs a clue?

Brains gone mushy from all the rays,
Pranking each other in funny ways.
I tried to dive, but belly-flopped,
A laugh attack—oh, how we dropped!

As day turns night, we gaze above,
With laughter, joy, and heaps of love.
Tomorrow's sun will rise again,
And we'll be here, just like, amen!

Celestial Warmth

The sun's so bright, it gives a wink,
We glide through life, not stopping to think.
With lemonade cups and silly hats,
We giggle loud with our sunbeam chats.

Each day is vibrant, each laugh is bright,
The stars come out, we dance with delight.
Camping out under the moon's embrace,
While critters join in this wild chase.

A fire pit crackles, roasting s'mores,
Sticky fingers and toasted scores.
We sing off-key, but hearts all soar,
In this joy, we could not ask for more.

As dawn breaks softly, dreams fade away,
But in our hearts, they always stay.
With rays of warmth that never tire,
We'll keep this laughter, our true desire.

Boundless Skies Above

In balloon hats, we fly and soar,
The sky's our playground, who needs a floor?
Kites tangled high, laughter takes flight,
Silly antics from morning to night.

Colorful sunsets paint the scene,
With faces beaming, we feel like queens.
Grass stains on knees from joyful runs,
These endless days are filled with puns.

A picnic spread with snacks galore,
Oops, I spilled juice! Just want some more.
Chasing fireflies, they're tricky and sly,
But we won't stop, we know we can fly!

The horizons call as stars come out,
We'll laugh together, that's what it's about.
These moments shine, forever bright,
Our hearts aglow, stars in the night.

Endless Tides of Joy

Sandy toes and ice cream cones,
Seagulls steal your potato scones.
Laughter bounces off the waves,
We dance like we're little knaves.

Flip-flops flying through the air,
Kites are tangled in your hair.
Sunburns shaped like silly smirks,
Perfect moments, no, just quirks.

Beachball battles with no war,
Splashing water, hear the roar!
Every sunbeam's like a friend,
In this joy that will not end.

So let the tide forever roll,
With every laugh, we feel more whole.
In this paradise, we laugh and play,
Chasing sunshine every day!

Eternal Embrace of Light

Sipping lemonade so sweet,
Watch that ant take on a treat.
Sunflowers wiggle with delight,
As we bask in warm sunlight.

Sunglasses on our noses bright,
We giggle at the passing sight.
Sunscreen battles on our skin,
Flops and flops, let's dive right in.

Our jokes float like dandelion seeds,
Tangled up in summer's deeds.
Furry friends join in the laugh,
Who knew grass could be a path?

As day blurs into the night,
Fireflies join our silly flight.
With every smile, we ignite,
Together in this endless light.

Eternal Sunshine

Bikini tops and board shorts worn,
Sunburnt noses, a life reborn.
As ice pops melt and drip away,
We giggle like it's yesterday.

Sun hats floating like balloons,
Dancing to the seasonal tunes.
Catching waves and jellybeans,
Life's a romp in silly scenes.

Sandcastle kings and queens we claim,
With moats of laughter, we exclaim.
Building dreams without a care,
In this sunny, blissful air.

So raise a glass to golden rays,
Where every moment's filled with plays.
In the warmth, our hearts align,
In this cheer, we brightly shine!

Days Without Twilight

Frying eggs on sidewalks, oh what glee,
Laugh along with your cup of tea.
Chasing clouds that seldom stay,
Daring shadows to come play.

Jumping waves and running free,
At the beach, it's you and me!
Radar pants and silly hats,
Did you see those stealthy cats?

Picnics on the ocean's edge,
With watermelon, we allege,
Days just slip in shades of fun,
We're all stars, we've just begun.

So sing aloud the sunny cheer,
In a world where laughter's near.
With every grin beneath the sky,
No more frowns, we're ever spry!

Seashells and Sunlight

On the beach, I found a shell,
Wearing a tiny, sandy Swell.
It whispered secrets to the breeze,
Said it dated a crab named Steve!

Sandcastles lean with a grin,
A moat for fish, they'll surely win.
Seagulls caw like a band gone wild,
Even the waves laugh like a child.

Flip-flops flop, a dance so sweet,
As my towel claims a sunlit seat.
I tried to sunbathe but just got burned,
Now I'm a lobster, lessons learned!

Ice cream drips with a silly plop,
Happiness melts, but I can't stop.
With every laugh, the day feels bright,
Living it up, from morn till night.

Sunlit Adventures

Chasing seagulls, me and my dog,
He runs for shells, I trip on a log.
We weave through sunbeams, wild and free,
Laughing with waves, just him and me.

A frisbee flies, oh what a catch,
But it lands straight – on a sunburned patch!
My friends all giggle, pointing out,
My fashion's now a lobsters' clout.

Carts of ice cream circle me,
I juggle cones with some bravado, see?
But two fall down, I laugh and say,
That's the price of a summer day!

With beach balls bouncing in the sand,
Our giggles rise, oh isn't it grand?
Each moment's joy under the sun,
These silly days, can't be outdone.

Glimmers of Forever

Footprints in sand, a quirky line,
Leading to ice cream, that's just divine!
I slipped on drizzle, what a surprise,
Now I'm the star, to everyone's eyes!

Shiny shells reflect the glee,
A dancing crab says, 'Dance with me!'
With every twirl, the tide applauds,
While my dog rolls in the sun, so flawed.

Kites overhead, in tangles they fight,
While I attempt to get it just right.
I'm a maestro of knots, full of flair,
Tangled in laughter, let down my hair.

Sunsets paint a canvas so bright,
With colors that dance, oh what a sight!
We'll haul our stories, strange and true,
Cuz these moments feel forever new.

Warmth in Every Breath

Sunglasses perched, I take a seat,
While kids run past with bare, sandy feet.
A beach ball lands with a playful thud,
Then bounces back, it's a family flood!

Waves tickle toes, as laughter flows,
There's magic here, everyone knows.
We build with dreams, our hearts alight,
Collecting wishes as day turns night.

Sipping lemonade, I spot a cat,
Stealing a shrimp from my picnic mat!
'Excuse me sir!' I only laugh,
As it struts away, a furry staff.

With each wave's crash, joy swells and grows,
This wild escape, a heart it sows.
The warmth we breathe, bright memories blend,
In sunlit spaces, fun never ends.

Sunlit Journeys

We packed our bags with sandals and fun,
Counting the days 'til we bask in the sun.
Ice cream drips down with a chuckle and cheer,
As seagulls squawk loud, 'Where's my snack, dear?'

The road ahead is lined in bright hues,
With beach balls bouncing and laughter ensues.
Sunscreen application, a comical task,
As one gets stuck like a white, gooey mask.

Bikini on backwards, we giggle and sway,
Lost in the music, we dance like ballet.
The sun sets slowly, with puns on our lips,
Creating our memories with joyful eclipse.

With each rising wave, our worries are tossed,
Building our castles, no matter the cost.
In this sunny place, our cares drift away,
Leaving us grinning, let's dance like we play.

Where Time Stands Still

In a world where clocks tick with a silly rhyme,
We stroll through the sands, unbothered by time.
Flip-flops in hand, we skip and we hop,
While jellyfish wave as we twirl and stop.

Seagulls debate who gets the last fry,
While kids build their dreams with a pie in the sky.
The weather is perfect, not a cloud in sight,
While all of our troubles take an unseen flight.

Sippin' on coconuts, our plans are askew,
As sunscreen replaces the drab with a hue.
We scribble our wishes on grains of soft sand,
Waiting for mermaids, to join our grand band.

As shadows grow long, our laughter will swell,
In a land without worries, where all is quite swell.
Let's share all our secrets, and sip on the thrill,
In this place of joy, where time stands so still.

Oceanic Embrace

Oh, the ocean grins, with a cheeky wave,
It invites us in for a splash and a rave.
With each playful poke from a gentle tide,
We squeal like children, with joy as our guide.

Surfboards in tow, we dance on the foam,
Floats become vessels, we feel so at home.
Our towels are picnic spots, sun hats all askew,
As we sip lemonade, in the sun's golden hue.

A crab in a tux makes his formal debut,
While fish in the deep play a game of peek-a-boo.
We're giggling like kids, what a sight to behold,
In a world full of wonders, our stories unfold.

So cheers to the waves, that tickle our feet,
In this oceanic land, life feels like a treat.
With laughter and joy that never rescinds,
Let the fun of the sea, become all that transcends.

Chasing Dawn

With sunrise a canvas, painted in flair,
We chase after dawn, with excitement to share.
Our coffee spills out as we gladly embrace,
The magic of morning, a rush of pure grace.

Sidewalks turn into runways, our feet all a-tap,
We skateboard and giggle, let's take a quick lap.
All the birds chirp songs that we can't help but sing,
As the world wakes up, we feel like a king.

In sun-kissed adventures, our minds take to flight,
As we laugh at the seagulls that steal our delight.
Frolicking freely, let's leave worries behind,
In this chase for dawn, new silliness we'll find.

With each passing moment, our spirits ignite,
Our hearts filled with joy, in morning's sweet light.
Together we'll wander through skies painted gold,
In search of fresh giggles, and stories retold.

The Sun's Sweet Refrain

The sun spills juice on the lawn,
Lemonade dreams, sipping till dawn.
A squirrel ballet, they twist and twirl,
While burgers sizzle in a smoky whirl.

Flip-flops flip on the picnic ground,
Ice cream drips, oh what a sound!
A sprinkle fight, laughter in the air,
As seagulls plot without a care.

Sunhats wobble with a funny flair,
Bobbling heads with sunblock to spare.
We giggle at clouds, a temporary pause,
As shadows whisper, we're marveled by flaws.

Naps underneath a big sunflower,
Dreaming of laughter, day's final hour.
The sun goes low, but spirits stay high,
Our endless joy, like stars in the sky.

Afternoon Delights

A garden party with mismatched chairs,
The cake's too big, no one really cares.
Hats askew in a constant breeze,
As bees plot to join in, if you please!

Water fights with chaotic cheers,
Drenched companions, no room for fears.
The dog steals burgers, what a sight,
Chasing his tail, he takes flight.

Whimsical clouds in a battle of hues,
Two kids argue, who gets the last juice?
Meanwhile, a crab wanders by with strut,
Pinching our fun—oh what a nut!

The sun nods low, a golden grin,
With laughter echoing, we all join in.
Stories are spun, like yarn on a loom,
This joy won't leave, it's too tough to broom.

Dreaming in Rays

Belly flops made a splashy sound,
The sun's big grin spreads all around.
Sunscreen slathered, we look like ghosts,
While dancing flames turn charcoal to toast.

A treasure map drawn in the sand,
For a chocolate bar, oh it's so grand!
Pirate wars break out, who's on the crew?
And who forgot to pack the blue goo?

Splashing puddles formed by the tide,
A crab scurries fast, it's quite a ride!
Mermaid tales, sung with a flair,
As seagulls judge from their lofty lair.

As evening settles its blanket of gold,
We share our stories, both new and old.
In these sweet rays, we find our hearts,
Crafting laughter, a million tiny parts.

A Realm of Everlasting Light

A kite flies high, lost in the blue,
While ice cream melts, we all scream, "Woo!"
Tents look like mushrooms in a fairy tale,
As we giggle and snack upon birthday kale.

The sandcastles rise, but oh, what a feat,
The waves are relentless with a watery greet.
A flip-flop missing, where could it be?
Dunked in the surf, it sighed, "Just let me be!"

Picnic ants parading on our spread,
Demanding a feast, we wish they were fed.
But who wouldn't share a donut or two?
When laughter's the treat shared by me and you!

As daylight dims, we gather near,
With marshmallows roasted and loud, cheerful cheer.
In this wacky world, sun hangs so bright,
We'll dance like shadows in the glowing twilight.

Endless Days at Dusk

Underneath the sun's warm glow,
We chase the shadows, to and fro.
With ice cream hats and flip-flop feet,
Laughter echoes down the street.

Jellybeans and lemonade,
We dance in puddles, unafraid.
The sandcastles wobble, but who cares?
Seagulls laugh, no time to spare.

Bright balloons float in the air,
A dog steals snacks; it's only fair.
As twilight brushes skies so blue,
We giggle, plan our next great brew.

Oh, how the days just slip away,
Like jellyfish on a summer bay.
We'll celebrate until the night,
Chasing stars, oh, what a sight!

A Tapestry of Light

Colors swirl in a dazzling dance,
Frisbees fly as if in trance.
With every laugh, the sunbeam sings,
Weird hats on heads, oh, what fun brings!

Picnic tables lined with treats,
Everyone's got mismatched seats.
Bugs invade, but we just swat,
Swapping stories, forgetting that!

The ice cream truck, we hear it chime,
We form a line, oh, every time!
A splash of sprinkles on our nose,
As fun-filled chaos ebbs and flows.

With every sunset, we create,
Memories that'll never fade.
Witty jokes and silly blunders,
Like magic spells, they pull our wonders.

Shoreline Echoes

Footprints in sand, we race the tide,
A beach ball fight, we laugh and hide.
With every wave, a salty kiss,
Who knew the ocean could be this bliss?

Sunblock smeared on our noses bright,
A squeaky toy joins in the fight.
Cooler opens – what will we munch?
Sandwiches, chips, and maybe a crunch.

Shells and treasures, we collect by hand,
Building castles, oh, isn't it grand?
A crab sidesteps with a daring sneer,
"Hey buddy, this is not your sphere!"

As twilight paints the scene with flair,
We sing and dance without a care.
The moon peeks in, a playful sprout,
Echoes of laughter, joy throughout.

Embrace of the Horizon

Bright sun hats and shades on deck,
We wave at clouds with hearty peck.
Kites soaring high, an airborne race,
Chasing the breeze with silly grace.

With laughter spilled across green hills,
Silly selfies, capturing thrills.
Bicycle bells go ding-a-ling,
As we hum our favorite spring fling.

With tacos and tunes for every taste,
We feast like kings, no time to waste.
A sunburnt nose and happy face,
Life's a party; let's quicken the pace!

As shadows stretch and colors fade,
We're superheroes in our escapade.
With memories bright, we head for home,
Stars guide the way – wherever we roam!

Sunrise to Sunset Reverie

The sun peeks out, a sleepy grin,
Wakes the world with a lazy spin.
Coffee spills, a clumsy dance,
Why does joy come with a chance?

We skip to the beach, laughter galore,
Tripping on towels, we tumble and roar.
Sunglasses crooked, stylishly blind,
Chasing seagulls, so poorly timed.

The picnic's a mess, chips in the sand,
Sandwiches fly from a clumsy hand.
Laughter erupts as we dodge the waves,
Every splash feels like summer saves.

As the sky blushes pink, day bids adieu,
We wave goodbye, but not to the brew.
For tomorrow we'll wake and do it all again,
In this twilight fun, where time knows no end.

The Glow of Infinite Skies

High above, the kite flies free,
Tangled in branches, oh woe is me!
Children laugh, stirring sweet ice cream,
While I chase clouds in a giggly dream.

The sun's a joker, hiding away,
Playing peekaboo through shades of gray.
Shadows dance, a silly parade,
As flip-flops squeak in the grand charade.

Hot dogs rolling, a frantic race,
Who knew they'd flee from this sunny place?
We catch them with laughter, a friendly race,
Living our best, with silly embrace.

As stars pop out in the evening's thread,
We sit in a circle, stories unread.
Laughter echoes, the moon shines bright,
In this whimsical glow, we find delight.

Boundless Beach Breezes

The wind's a prankster, tugs at our hats,
Sending us soaring, just like the cats.
Beach balls collide with giggles so loud,
While sunscreen splatters on a proud crowd.

Shells scatter, as we run on the shore,
Counting odd shells, who could ask for more?
The sand between toes starts to chime,
In the rhythm of fun, we're losing track of time.

Ice cream drips more than we can devour,
Just like our dreams, sweet summer power.
We make sandcastles, while laughter erupts,
And chase the tide, feeling so abrupt.

As the sun bows down, painting the scene,
We revel in chaos, idyllic and serene.
With a wink to tomorrow, we shout with glee,
In this carnival breeze, we're wild and free.

Dreaming Under Azure Canopies

Under a blue sky, we lay on the grass,
Counting the clouds, as moments pass.
One looks like a rabbit, bright and spry,
While another's a boat sailing on high.

We share our secrets with the buzzing bees,
Trading giggles with the rustling trees.
Each breeze whispers tales that make us grin,
Chasing sunlight, where adventures begin.

A game of tag through light and shade,
Stepping on daisies, never afraid.
A sandwich squished, laughter ensues,
As we feast on memories, picturesque views.

When twilight kisses the day goodbye,
Fireflies wink in the indigo sky.
With dreams in our hearts, tomorrow will gleam,
Under azure canopies, we continue to dream.

Infinity in Every Ray

Bikini tan lines, a map of my day,
Lemonade laughs in the sun's bright ballet.
Flip-flops are squeaking, the seagulls prance,
Life is a beach, come join the dance!

A dork in sunglasses, strike a cool pose,
Count sand in my toes, how funny it grows!
Sunburned noses, we giggle and sigh,
Why must ice cream always just fly?

Waves crashing gently, a salty embrace,
Sunscreen smears, I become a new face.
Catch a crab dancing, oh look, it's alive!
A sunset can't stop us, we'll always survive!

So here's to the moments we cherish with glee,
Under skies painted bright, wild and free.
With laughter and giggles that frame our long days,
We find our infinity in sunshine's rays.

Sweet Summer Dances

Breezy skirts spinning, the warm air does sway,
Ice-cream cone juggling, oh what a display!
Mosquitoes are buzzers, the party's alive,
While flip-flops are dancing, and so do we thrive.

Picnic mishaps with juice on the floor,
Watermelon seeds flying, we laugh and we roar.
Spinning in circles on a ferris wheel high,
Screams turn to giggles as we float to the sky.

Funky sun hats tipping, we strut down the street,
Chasing the ice cream truck, that magical beat.
Silly selfies taken, we capture our smiles,
All smiles invigorated, it stretches for miles.

We dance through the days with the sun all aglow,
Creating our fun under nature's bright show.
With memories crafted, like ties we won't sever,
These sweet summer dances, oh joy, oh forever!

Unfading Sunsets

The sun takes a bow, painted pink on the sky,
But here comes a soccer ball flying right by.
We dive for the win, trip over our own,
Laughter erupting—the true prize we own.

Picnic blanket spread, sandwiches flop,
Ants are holding a meeting, make haste to swap!
The cooler is empty, but we cheer and chime,
In this goofy moment, it's the best of our time.

Bright pastels blooming, the colors collide,
Chasing those fireflies with friends by our side.
We wave at the sky, oh what a delight,
These unfading sunsets—the funniest sight!

So gather your stories, your smiles, your cheer,
Embrace every moment, don't shed a tear.
We'll dance into twilight, with spirits so high,
In the warm fading colors, we love and we fly.

Echoes of Sunlit Laughter

Running through sprinklers, it's splash time again,
With silly squirt flowers, we're warriors of rain!
Sun-kissed and wet, we can't stop the glee,
Echoes of laughter, it's a summer decree.

Popsicles melting, sticking to hands,
We wear rainbow shirts made from simple plans.
Oh, the joy of the puddles, let's stomp with a cheer,
Each splash a reminder that fun's always near.

Picking wildflowers and making a crown,
Pretending we're queens while we twirl all around.
Silly old turtles can't keep up the pace,
In this magical summer, we find our own space.

So gather your friends, and let's play till it's night,
Chasing echoes of laughter, it feels so right.
With sun-kissed adventures that never run dry,
In this season of joy, we'll forever comply!

www.ingramcontent.com/pod-product-compliance
Lightning Source LLC
Chambersburg PA
CBHW072133070526
44585CB00016B/1651